Whispers of the Willow

In the garden where willows sway,
A squirrel performs in a comical way.
He flips and he hops, what a sight!
Chasing his shadow with all of his might.

The branches giggle, a rustling tune,
As bees start to dance, under the moon.
The breeze joins in, with a cheeky grin,
Tickling the leaves, where fun does begin.

Serenade of Sturdy Roots

Roots intertwining, a bold ballet,
Twirling and swirling, they frolic and play.
They trip over stones, and giggle aloud,
Creating a jig that draws quite a crowd.

The earthworms cheer, they clap in delight,
As daisies join in for the evening's invite.
With laughter and mirth, they sway in the glen,
Nature's own party, once and again.

Echoes in the Canopy

Up in the treetops, the owls are wise,
But even they chuckle at the bats' surprise.
They swoop and they dive in a dizzying chase,
A misstep here, oh what a funny face!

The rustling leaves hold their breath so tight,
As branches play tag, from morning to night.
Whispered giggles float down with the breeze,
Turning the forest into a laugh spree.

The Lullaby of Leafy Shelters

Crickets sing softly, a melody sweet,
While the rabbits hop to the thump of their feet.
Twirling 'round mushrooms, they dance in a line,
Each leap a tickle, pure joy so divine!

The trees look on, with a wink and a sway,
As raccoons come out to join in the play.
Under the stars, in a twinkle and cheer,
They celebrate life, with laughter sincere.

Canine Echoes at Twilight

In twilight's glow, a tail does wag,
A chorus of barks, they joyously brag.
The squirrels tune in, the trees they sway,
As playful pups frolic and prance away.

With jowls all slack, and eyes wide bright,
They leap and dance into the night.
A canine choir, what a silly sight,
As shadows frolic, with pure delight.

Harmonies of the Hidden Grove

In a secret spot where the doggos play,
They bark in harmony, come what may.
The bushes shake with their merry sound,
As squirrels take flight, they leap and bound.

A pitiful howler, trying to sing,
Finds it unclear just what joy does bring.
Yet laughter echoes through leafy bends,
As playful antics become good friends.

Barking in the Moonlight

Beneath the moon, they raise their call,
With joyous howls that seem to enthrall.
The cats look down from their lofty perch,
While laughter dances within the lurch.

A pup takes charge, leading the pack,
With woofs and yaps, they never lack.
They prance and pounce on shadows' plays,
Creating mischief on starry bays.

Odes to the Old Oak

By the grand old tree, their spirits rise,
With goofy grins and playful sighs.
They chase each other, tails in a whirl,
Barking tunes that make their hearts twirl.

The oak stands tall, a witness engaged,
To every bark as day turns to stage.
A finale of yips, and then a bow,
As the sun dips low, they take a vow.

Serenade of the Sunlit Grove

In the grove where giggles play,
Squirrels dance and squirrels sway.
They toss acorns, joke and glide,
Each leafy laugh a sweet delight.

Sunlight casts a golden glow,
As rabbits hop and shadows grow.
A feathered choir sings a tune,
While frogs croak rhythms with the moon.

Hilarity in rustling leaves,
The winds weave in, no one grieves.
Each branch a stage, each root a chair,
Nature's jesters without a care.

Oh what fun, amidst the trees,
Where laughter floats upon the breeze!
Through branches low and skies so blue,
Joyful jesters shine anew.

The Bark of the Storyteller

In the woods where stories blend,
Trees gossip, they twist and bend.
With roots that wiggle, trunks that sway,
They share tall tales throughout the day.

Old Oak whispers bad dad jokes,
While Treetop laughs and pokes fun hoax.
The wind it chuckles through the leaves,
As happy tales weave and interweaves.

Underneath, a squirrel is brave,
He teases friends by acting cave.
With every bark, a punchline found,
The forest echoes with merry sound.

Sticks can talk, just wait and see,
Each knotted branch has wit, oh glee!
Grab a seat, feel free to stay,
In this merry wood, hear the play.

Poetic Paws of the Past

In shadows tall where paws have roamed,
A cheeky cat found tales well honed.
With every step, a legacy,
Her purring rhymes, a melody.

An old dog dreams of days gone by,
With wagging tail and sparkling eye.
He tells of chases, of love so pure,
His bark a tune, his heart the lure.

Each paw print holds a silly jest,
Stories bloom where laughter's blessed.
From chasing tails to midnight spies,
Adventure sprouts 'neath starry skies.

Oh, gather round, come hear the fun,
Each fluffy tale just shines like sun.
The past is full of frolic and cheer,
With furry friends, the laughter's near!

Whispers Beneath the Boughs

Beneath the boughs where shadows play,
The winds spin stories day by day.
Silly whispers flutter free,
Each tale wrapped round a giggling tree.

Chipmunks chat, with tiny grins,
Exchanging secrets like old kin.
They talk of acorns, laugh at rain,
With each new jest, they spark a gain.

A sleepy owl will wink an eye,
As playful deer go bounding by.
The forest dances, full of cheer,
Every sound brings laughter near.

So take a seat, let laughter flow,
Join in the tales, let humor grow.
Beneath the boughs, the joy extends,
In nature's arms, where joy transcends.

Chants from the Woodland Floor

In the midst of grassy hue,
Squirrels sing a silly tune,
With nuts stacked high, they'll rendezvous,
Underneath the playful moon.

Frogs leap high with croaky laughs,
Chasing fireflies in the night,
Their hoppy dance, a joke that halves,
The peace of nature's gentle light.

Rhythms Beneath the Boughs

Bees are buzzing, oh so bright,
Doing the tango, what a sight!
With flowery hats and tiny shoes,
They groove along, spreading the news.

The owls hoot with such great flair,
Dressed in wisdom, none can compare,
As rabbits hop, they twist and twirl,
In woodland halls, they spin and swirl.

Harmonies of Twisted Branches

The branches sway with whispered tales,
Each leaf is dancing, none that fails,
In the wind they play a tune,
Of juggling acorns and silver spoons.

The raccoons clap with furry paws,
Underneath the stars, they pause,
Sharing giggles, apple pie,
As owls wink at passersby.

Nature's Poetic Embrace

A playful gust, it tickles trees,
With swaying limbs, they dance with ease,
While chipmunks chatter, making schemes,
Their giggles float on sunlit beams.

With every rustle, laughter grows,
As flowers bloom, their colors glow,
In this realm of silly cheer,
Nature's heart beats loud and clear.

Cadences in the Canopy

In the trees where squirrels play,
Chasing shadows, bright as day.
Each acorn drops like tiny drums,
Making music, oh so fun!

Birds join in with chirps and calls,
Spreading joy as nature sprawls.
A symphony of leaf and breeze,
Whispers through the swaying trees.

A Rhapsody for the Rover

A dog with dreams of chasing tails,
Dancing 'neath the sunlit trails.
His paws a blur, he makes a dash,
While birds scream out in fits of flash.

With every bark, he steals the scene,
Bounding forth, a joyous bean.
The world's a stage for him to rule,
An endearing, goofy fool.

Verses of the Verdant Vale

In the vale where daisies grow,
A rabbit hops and steals the show.
With floppy ears and eyes so bright,
He leaps and twirls, what a sight!

The flowers giggle in the sun,
As bees buzz round, having fun.
A picnic spreads beneath the sky,
And laughter dances, oh so spry.

Poised in the Pine's Embrace

Beneath the pines, a squirrel nurds,
Crafting tales in flurries and spurts.
With nuts aplenty, he starts to plot,
A feast for friends, and oh, what a lot!

The winds join in with gentle roars,
Rustling leaves like open doors.
In this realm of laughter and play,
Nature sings out, come what may.

Timberline Twilight Tunes

As twilight falls, the trees do sway,
Squirrels dance in a curious way.
A twig plays bass, a leaf sings high,
Under the stars, the crickets sigh.

A raccoon taps on a hollow log,
While owls hoot like a wise old dog.
The moonlight whispers with a funny glee,
Nature's stage, for all to see.

Beneath the pines, a melody free,
The wind joins in, oh, what a spree!
Giggles and chuckles in the cool night air,
Life's a jest, beyond compare.

So raise a toast, with acorns and pine,
To forest tunes that brightly shine.
In this crowd of critters, each outlandish soul,
Strumming the chords, feeling whole.

The Coyote's Cadence

Under the moon, coyotes howl,
Their serenade makes the night prowl.
A little fox joins with a jig on the side,
Wagging his tail, full of pride.

The pack harmonizes, each voice a flare,
A raucous riddle floats through the air.
Dancing shadows, like a lively quest,
Sudden chaos, it's quite the jest!

With each flick of a paw and twist of a tail,
They sing of mischief, the wind in their sail.
As moonlight glints on their playful charade,
The forest echoes with laughter displayed.

So when you hear that wild refrain,
Join in the frolic, let go of your pain.
For in every yelp and playful tease,
Lies the true spirit of nature's ease.

Notes from Nature's Choir

In a leafy glade, the birds strike up,
With chirps and trills, a joyful cup.
Each little note a playful jest,
Nature's symphony at its best.

A beehive hums, a buzzing tune,
While butterflies twirl, dancing in June.
The turtles bop to a rhythm slow,
With a sprinkle of laughter, to and fro.

As frogs jump in with a sudden croak,
It's a ribbiting moment, the sweetest joke.
The squirrels chime in with their chatter and glee,
Nature's concert, wild and free!

So come, take part in this voicing spree,
Where even the wind joins in with glee.
With leaves as instruments, let worries flee,
In this nature choir, we all sing with glee.

Melody of the Main Trail

On the main trail, footsteps go thump,
With shadows dancing, giving a jump.
A raccoon struts with an air of sass,
Calling out friends from the tall, sweet grass.

The rustling leaves played soft and low,
As laughter bubbled from below.
Woodpeckers drum on an old oak tree,
Creating a beat that sets spirits free.

A jogger stumbles, laughing surprised,
Even the pinecones have candid eyes.
The path winds on with a comical plot,
Nature's funhouse, give it a shot!

So hike along, let your worries pale,
In the melody found on the winding trail.
For every twist brings a hearty cheer,
In the forest's song, there's nothing to fear.

Verse of the Venerable Cedar

In the woods where the old trees stand,
A squirrel plays with a nut in hand.
He vaults through branches, what a sight!
Chasing shadows, day and night.

The wise old oak just shakes his leaves,
Telling tales of mischief that deceives.
While the pine needles giggle with glee,
At the antics of friends in the tree.

A raccoon rolls down with a giggly shout,
Searching for snacks, he's never in doubt.
With a wiggle and jiggle, quite the show,
In the heart of the forest, off he'll go!

Oh, the laughter rings from each tree's crown,
As critters conspire, no time for a frown.
So join in the fun, let your spirit soar,
In the jubilant woods, you'll find so much more!

The Testimony of the Timberland

The trees lean in with a chuckle to share,
Whispers of laughter hang thick in the air.
A rabbit jigs with a floppy sidebar,
Rhythms in nature echo near and far.

With a thud! Comes the bear, a clumsy king,
Tripping on roots, what joy does he bring!
He scratches his belly and yawns in the sun,
While the birds tweet loudly, 'Aren't we all fun?'

The breeze carries tales from the highest branch,
Of critters in costumes who love to dance.
From acorns to capers, they leap and they twirl,
In this timberland circus, let your mind whirl!

In the shade of the trees, laughter unfolds,
Where stories of joy and mischief are told.
Stay for a while, stay on the trail,
In the heart of the timber, let joy prevail!

Whispers in the Canopy

Up above in the leafy realm,
Canaries are singing, joy at the helm.
With wings so bright, they tickle the air,
Spreading giggles from here to there.

The clever raccoon dons a hat made of leaves,
Planning a prank while the squirrel he grieves.
His stash is now claimed by a plucky young fox,
Who dances around, while the woodpecker knocks.

Beneath chattering branches, a ticklish breeze,
Caresses the ferns with mischief and ease.
They curl up and giggle, they sway with delight,
As whispers of laughter fill up the night.

So climb up high, let your spirits bounce,
Feel the joy in nature, one shouldn't renounce.
In the canopy's embrace, let mirth multiply,
Join the chorus of laughter, just give it a try!

Echoes of the Forest Floor

Among the roots where the shadows do play,
A playful fox starts his hide-and-seek day.
With a wink and a wiggle, he scampers about,
While the mushrooms chuckle, about their new route.

The critters are gathered beneath the old tree,
Creating a symphony, wild and carefree.
They tap dance on twigs, what a splendid affair,
With ticks from the toads announcing they're there!

As light filters down through the twisty old limbs,
The earth whispers back in harmonious hymns.
Laughter erupts from the burrows below,
With every new jest, they steal the show!

Join the joyous ensemble, come catch a good laugh,
In this merry woodland, where happiness quaffs.
Through echoes of merriment, hearts will grow bold,
In the magic of the forest, let your spirit unfold!

The Canine Chorus

In the park where dogs all meet,
They sing and dance on happy feet.
Chasing tails and barking loud,
A furry and boisterous crowd.

Squeaky toys are their delight,
Barking songs from morn till night.
With wags and leaps, they take the stage,
A canine show, pure doggone rage.

Each pup adds their special tune,
Underneath the silver moon.
A symphony of playful barks,
Echoing through the neighborhood parks.

Starlit Howls

Under twinkling stars above,
The hounds engage in songs of love.
Howling softly, they share their dreams,
While chasing shadows, bursting seams.

One spots a cat and strikes a pose,
With tail a-wag and nose it goes.
The moonlight catches all the fun,
As pups unite, 'til night is done.

In their chorus, laughter swells,
A howl, a bark, the midnight bells.
As if the night itself would play,
A symphony till break of day.

Rhythm of the Woodland

In the woods where creatures roam,
The critters sing of their sweet home.
With scratches, nibbles, barks, and peeps,
They dance on paws in merry leaps.

Squirrels chatter, birds collide,
The forest floor becomes their pride.
Puppies prance with wild delight,
Underneath the dappled light.

Each rustle brings a new surprise,
From playful growls to searching eyes.
In harmony, they weave their lore,
As laughter echoes evermore.

Timber Tales and Tails

Wooden logs and furry friends,
Cuddly chaos that never ends.
With wagging tails that tell a tale,
They scamper off, they never fail.

One digs deep, the other spins,
A rollicking dance of furry grins.
In every nook and cranny explored,
A new adventure, never bored.

Beneath the pines, they climb and trot,
In search of mischief, they love a lot.
Their laughter rings through trees so tall,
These merry mutts, they've got it all.

Whistling Woods and Wags

In the woods where the tall trees sway,
A squirrel prances, it thinks it can play.
With a jump and a twist, it takes a bold leap,
But a dog with a sniff just wants his sweet sleep.

The raccoons gather, plotting their theft,
While the owl hoots softly, a wise little heft.
They dance round the trunk, not knowing the tale,
Of the pup 'neath the shade, dreaming without fail.

A fox joins the fun, with a flick of its tail,
Chasing shadows of branches, on a whimsical trail.
The others all giggle, they trip and they fall,
In the comedy show of the whistling woods' hall.

As the sun dips low, their laughter does throng,
Who knew trees could Hold such a humorous song?
In the echoing twilight, they yip and they brawl,
The nightly escapade, a brisk, furry ball.

A Melody of Leaves and Licks

Leaves whisper secrets, all green and amused,
As a pup in the grass lays sharply confused.
With a flick of his tongue, he licks the bright air,
While butterflies giggle, fluttering without care.

He spins in circles, a dizzying plight,
Chasing his own tail, oh what a sight!
The flowers all chuckle, they sway with delight,
As his antics unfold, pure joy in the light.

A breeze carries notes of a playful old tune,
Humming through branches beneath the bright moon.
The dog howls along, with his goofy refrain,
As a chorus of crickets joins in the gain.

As dusk kindly settles, the fun doesn't cease,
With wags and with wiggles, they all find their peace.
A melody woven of leaves and of licks,
Nature's own laughter, a canvas of tricks.

Nightfall's Node

In the stillness of night, strange shadows do glide,
A cat with a strut thinks it's smart to decide.
It prances so sly, but a dog's snore erupts,
And the cat jumps a mile, in a twist it interrupts.

The moonlight's a spotlight, on nature's own stage,
While a hedgehog rolls by like a tiny, mad sage.
The laughter of owls fills the night with a cheer,
As they watch the antics, both timeless and dear.

A raccoon steals snacks, with a mask on its face,
But the dog's found the goods, leading a wild chase.
Through bushes and brambles, they scamper and scheme,
In this nighttime ballet, a wonderfully silly dream.

When morning breaks softly, with a giggle or two,
The critters all gather and share what they knew.
In the whispers of night, where all creatures play,
They plot their next episode at the close of the day.

Songs of the Silent Shadows

In the corners of dusk, where the shadows all blend,
A poodle in pink finds her day at an end.
She prances on tiptoes, so graceful, so bold,
But slips on a leaf... what a sight to behold!

The moon peeks around, like a shy little kid,
At the pup's brave ballet, oh what a great bid!
With a tumble and roll, she bounces back up,
While the laughter of crickets begins to erupt.

Then a determined old badger appears in this tale,
With a waddle so charming, but it's missing its tail.
The dog cocks her head, with a curious gleam,
As the badger walks by, lost in its own dream.

The night wraps around them, a cool, gentle cover,
While they sing of their adventures, one after another.
In the silence of shadows, the fun does unfold,
With songs that delight, in the twilight's soft hold.

The Whispering Woodlands

In the woods where squirrels jest,
A raccoon wears a dapper vest.
The trees gossip in the breeze,
While owls hoot jokes with ease.

The mushrooms giggle at the ants,
Who dance about in funny pants.
A deer prances with a twist,
While nearby, the rabbits list.

The winds carry laughter high,
As butterflies flutter by.
All creatures share a quirky grin,
In a world where silliness begins.

From branch to branch, the tales fly,
Of silly stunts that make you sigh.
In this woodland of delight,
Funny antics bring pure light.

A Symphony of Snouts

In a meadow, snouts abound,
With piglets playing all around.
A chorus of snuffles fills the air,
As puppies join the wild affair.

Goats sing tunes with mighty glee,
While chickens cluck in harmony.
A rabbit's solo, quite the sight,
With waltzing steps, both bold and bright.

A symphony of noses met,
In a concert that's hard to forget.
With horns and hooves in funny dance,
Every critter gets a chance!

When evening falls, the show must end,
But laughter echoes, like an old friend.
In the barn where the snouts unite,
The joy lingers long into the night.

Legends of the Leafy Glen

In the glen where leaves do twirl,
A hedgehog spins in quite a whirl.
Tales of bravery run amok,
Like the rabbit that outsmarted a rock.

The shadows dance, as fables speak,
Of cheeky foxes with tricks so sleek.
The wise old owl, perched up high,
Chuckles softly with a knowing sigh.

With every rustle, a new tale grows,
Of dancing badgers and silly crows.
An acorn drops and makes a splash,
As laughter fills the leafy clash.

It's a pocket of whimsy, pure delight,
Where legends thrive in the soft starlight.
In the leafy glen, all joy runs free,
Crafting tales of silly jubilee.

Sonnet of the Serene Stream

By the stream where ripples play,
A frog leaps forth in a splashy way.
Each jump a giggle, a hop so grand,
It croaks a tale of a wobbly band.

The fish below giggle and tease,
As dragonflies dance, quite at ease.
A turtle winks with a wise old grin,
As if to say, "Let the fun begin!"

With laughter bubbling in the flow,
The stream shares secrets, fast and slow.
Mirth and joy are our daily theme,
In the happy waltz of the serene stream.

As twilight falls on this lively scene,
Nature serenades, sweet and keen.
A gentle mix of whimsy and cheer,
Where every moment feels like a souvenir.

The Sylvan Symphony

In the woods the canines prance,
Their tails a-wag in wild romance.
With each leap they chase a squirrel,
A symphony of fur in whirl.

Leaves rain down like nature's cheer,
While pups just bark without a fear.
They serenade the passing breeze,
A funny tune among the trees.

Squirrels tease with acorn delight,
As dogs dance 'round with purest might.
Their paws tap time upon the ground,
In this sweet forest play, they're found.

When night falls soft, they curl and snooze,
While moonlight casts enchanting hues.
A gentle whimper, a cozy sigh,
Tomorrow's fun is just nearby.

Barking Ballads at Dusk

As twilight spreads its dusky veil,
The dogs break into a howling tale.
A moonlit chorus, loud and spry,
With barks that echo through the sky.

Each note a chase, each bark a cheer,
A comedy of canines, oh so near.
The owl hoots back, a wise old friend,
In laughter and music, the fun won't end.

With tails held high and sniffles grand,
They compose a symphony of land.
Through trees they run, through paths they play,
Their jolly ballads welcome the day.

At last they rest beneath the stars,
Dreaming of adventures and candy bars.
With dreams of bones and frisbees, too,
They snooze till dawn, when skies turn blue.

Dog Days and Woodsy Ways

In summer woods, the pups convene,
Amongst the trees, they live the dream.
With yips and yaps, they share their tales,
Of treasure hunts and happy trails.

A splash in streams, they leap and bound,
Chasing shadows across the ground.
Their laughter rings in barks and yowls,
As bugs and critters play the fowls.

With sticks in jaws, they proudly stride,
Each moment's joy, they never hide.
A gentle nudge or playful bite,
It's woodsy fun from morn till night.

As sun sinks low, they gather near,
Swapping stories, no hint of fear.
In dreams they soar, through piney views,
As daylight fades, the fun ensues.

Lullabies of the Leaves

As breezes hum a gentle tune,
The dogs lay down, their eyes like moons.
With leaves that dance in playful flight,
They dream of joy through starry night.

A rustle here, a whisper there,
In doggy dreams, there's fluff and flair.
A game of chase with moonlit barks,
And teddy bears beneath the larks.

With sleepy tails and snores so sweet,
The forest hums a soft retreat.
They snuggle close in nature's keep,
As crickets sing them off to sleep.

The lullabies of leaves nearby,
Keep watch over each sleepy sigh.
A funny dream, of mischievous ways,
Till morning light brings new dog days.

Sonnet of the Sunlit Clearing

In the glade where shadows play,
Squirrels debate their acorn way.
Old leaves whisper tales so bright,
While sunlight dances, pure delight.

The owls hoot their nightly cheer,
As rabbits hop without a fear.
With butterflies in zig-zag flight,
They frolic 'til the end of light.

Yet watch the grass, it starts to sway,
A tickle fight begins, hooray!
A game of jest beneath the pines,
Where laughter springs like swirling vines.

Oh sunlit clearing, full of glee,
Your joyful spirit's wild and free.
Here in the woods, we break the gloom,
A raucous tune in nature's room.

Poems Written in Petals

On petals soft, I write my verse,
In colors bright, I feel immersed.
A bee hums tunes, unaware of jest,
While flowers giggle, feeling blessed.

The daisies chant a silly rhyme,
They sway and sway, oh what a time!
A butterfly, with pompous flair,
Pretends it's royalty in the air.

I add a line about the breeze,
Which tickles leaves like playful tease.
A dandelion starts to spin,
And blows a wish for fun to win.

So here's my ode to blooms so fine,
With colors mixing, so sublime.
In gardens rich with life we sing,
With petals sweet, our joy takes wing.

Resonance of the Rustic Path

Upon the path where rabbits race,
Uneven stones mark out the space.
The squirrels chatter, full of sass,
As they watch friends take a tumble, alas!

With every step, the leaves now crack,
A wise old tortoise gives us flack.
He grumbles low, in slow but sure,
While flowers laugh, their joy is pure.

A billy goat, with utmost pride,
Makes quite an entrance, takes a stride.
He bleats a tune, off-key yet grand,
In this rustic land, all things are planned.

So wander forth, embrace the fun,
In nature's play, we all are one.
With laughter mixed in every breath,
The rustic path beats back all stress.

The Ode of the Overarching Canopy

Beneath the boughs where shadows loom,
The critters plot a grand costume.
With acorn hats and leafy cloaks,
They scheme and dream like silly folks.

A parrot squawks a cheeky joke,
While munching seeds, through laughter choked.
The branches shimmy in delight,
As friends unite beneath the light.

Oh canopy, so vast and wide,
In your embrace, we laugh and glide.
A raccoon dances, twirls with flair,
Beckoning all to join the air.

So raise a cheer for leafy shade,
Where silly antics can't evade.
In nature's hug, we find our song,
With every giggle, we belong.

Fables of the Flora and Fauna

In a garden lived a gossiping flower,
Whispering tales in the morning hour.
A bee flew by, buzzing loud and proud,
"Shhh! Don't say that, or we'll draw a crowd!"

The ants held a conference, dressed in suits,
Discussing the latest in leafy pursuits.
"My leaf's the best," the young sprout proclaimed,
While an old vine chuckled, "Oh, how we've changed!"

A snail wrote a letter, took hours to send,
Addressed to the grass, his very best friend.
"It's slow and steady that wins in the race,
But I'll let you know when I pick up the pace!"

So the plants continued, with humor and cheer,
Where laughter and antics would fill the whole sphere.
In the heart of the garden, they thrived and they leaped,
In tales of the flora, the secrets they keep.

Chords of the Crescendoing Seasons

As spring made an entrance with a splash of delight,
The robins were singing, oh what a sight!
A squirrel in tights danced atop a tall fence,
While flowers joined in, feeling quite dense.

Summer rolled in, with sun beams that play,
A cricket created a grand cabaret.
While frogs hopped along with a beat in their feet,
And fireflies twinkled, feeling the heat.

Autumn arrived with a rustling sound,
The leaves did a waltz, swirling around.
A hedgehog in plaid, very dapper and neat,
Sipped on hot cocoa, quite the cute treat.

Then winter looked in, with frost on the land,
A snowman jiggled as the snowflakes were planned.
"Hold on!" he exclaimed, in a humorous cheer,
"Let's make this a party, I'll invite all the deer!"

So seasons collided in laughter and thrill,
Every chord played a note, each moment a thrill.
With joy overflowing from nature's sweet song,
The chords of the seasons would always belong.

The Epic of the Erudite Oak

In a glade stood an oak, wise beyond years,
Telling tales to the breeze, and conquering fears.
The squirrels held lectures, taking keen notes,
While owls wore glasses, pondering quotes.

"Why do leaves rustle?" a young sprite did question,
The oak chuckled gently, giving a lesson.
"'Tis the whispers of wisdom," he said with a grin,
"Nature's own gossip, let the fun begin!"

A raccoon in bowtie offered a play,
"Let's act out your stories, in a quirky way!"
The creatures all gathered, applause filled the air,
As the million-branch tale turned into a square.

With laughter and jest, the forest came alive,
Every creature joined in, with joy to survive.
So the oak stood tall, and his legends took flight,
An epic of fun, from morn till the night.

Murmurs in the Meadow

In the meadow, whispers floated like the breeze,
A bunny told secrets beneath the tall trees.
"Did you hear about Freddy, the fella with hops?
He danced with a toad, and forgot all the stops!"

The flowers giggled, with petals a-sway,
"Just yesterday, Gerald caught a bee in his hay.
He tried to make friends, ended up with a sting,
Now he's cautious with buzzers, it's a real zany thing!"

A grasshopper leaped, sharing tales of delight,
"Last night the moon also tripped, what a sight!
I swear I could hear her laugh through the stars,
As she rolled in her shimmer, escaping her scars."

So the meadow oozed with stories to share,
Of critters and laughter, festival flair.
Where murmurs of joy carried high on the wind,
In scenes of pure fun, where the laughter won't end.

Fables from the Furrows

In the fields, a cow sang loud,
While chickens danced, drawing a crowd.
A pig in boots did pirouettes,
As fields filled up with giggling pets.

A sheep recited poems so slick,
While goats played cards, oh what a trick!
The horse wore glasses, looked quite wise,
As laughter echoed 'neath blue skies.

The corn stalks swayed with a joyous cheer,
As all gathered 'round to lend an ear.
With tales of old and jokes anew,
The animals know just what to do.

So if you wander where the fields are wide,
You'll find the joy they can't abide.
Each tale a twist, each laugh a sound,
In furrowed fables, fun is found!

Paw Prints and Prose

A dog named Rex wrote tales of treats,
Of sneaky cats and running feats.
His paws would scratch across the page,
While gossip soared, like we're on stage.

The turtle chimed with a slow, wise grin,
"It's not the rush, it's the fun within!"
The parakeet squawked, "Oh dear, oh my!"
As squirrels played tag, running by.

A chorus rose from the bouncy hounds,
With silly songs and woofs that astound.
Through prose they danced, their spirits high,
In the world of paws, there's no goodbye.

So grab a treat and bring a friend,
Let's twirl in stories that never end.
For every tale, there's joy to spare,
With paw prints and prose, we spread good cheer!

Chorus of the Canopy

In the treetops, the monkeys swing,
With banter loud, they laugh and sing.
A parrot dined on a fruity snack,
While squirrels schemed for a bold squirrel hack.

A wise old owl, perched on a limb,
Told tales of woe with a humorous whim.
"Whooo says I'm wise? It's just my hat!"
And down below, a raccoon sat.

With roots and leaves they formed a band,
As laughter danced across the land.
Each note was met with a chirp or two,
In the canopy where fun ensues.

So join the throng, let your giggles flow,
Beneath the greens, let your joy grow.
In the chorus of trees, with laughter sweet,
Find the rhythm of joy and beat!

Songs of the Squirrel

A squirrel with cheeks packed full of nuts,
Sang tunes so catchy, made all the cuts.
With leaps and bounds, he stole the show,
While nutty friends joined in the flow.

A rabbit clapped, with ears so tall,
As hedgehogs spun and began to crawl.
"Don't eat my stash!" cried the squirrel bold,
"Or you'll miss the tales that are yet to be told!"

From trunk to trunk, they made their way,
In a frolicsome dance, come what may.
Each verse a giggle, every laugh a cheer,
In the songs of the squirrels, there's nothing to fear.

So if you find yourself in the woods so bright,
Listen close for their songs, what a delight!
With each bounding leap, let laughter unfold,
In the tales of the squirrels, be young and bold!

The Ballad of the Burgeoning Blossoms

In the garden, petals dance with glee,
Worms throw parties under the big tree.
Bees wear hats, buzzing a song,
As ladybugs jive to the beats all day long.

Sunshine sprinkles, a golden shower,
Flowers gossip, sharing their power.
'Look at me!' one says with a twist,
As butterflies flutter, they can't resist.

Tall trees chuckle, their branches shake,
Squirrels race for the best cream cake.
With each bloom, a quirky tale,
Of laughter hidden in every trail.

Portraits in the Bark's Embrace

Trees wear faces, carved in delight,
Gnarled old oaks chuckle in the night.
Silly squirrels peek from their homes,
Dressed like poets, reciting their tomes.

As shadows dance, the branches sway,
A raccoon's solo steals the play.
Laughter echoes, a woodsy choir,
Of creatures aiming to never tire.

Each scar on the bark tells a jest,
Of foolish foxes and their silly quest.
Green leaves giggle in the soft breeze,
Reminding us all that joy's like trees.

Rhymes of the Rooted Souls

Roots wiggle, an underground dance,
Earthworms tango, given the chance.
A stumpy beetle beats on the ground,
While ants form conga lines all around.

Laughter erupts from the leafy thrones,
As tiny critters hum silly tones.
Mossy carpets, a plush embrace,
In the forest, life's a funny race.

Hello, goodbye, the trees just grin,
As flowers bloom and then fade, thin.
Nature's secrets, they chuckle and tease,
Rhymes from the depths wrap us with ease.

The Narrative of Nature's Canvass

Across the canvas, colors collide,
A splatter of purple, green, and fried.
Giggles arise from the creek's flow,
As fish flip over, putting on a show.

The sun paints stories on clouds so bright,
While shadows play hide and seek at night.
A laughing crow cracks a joke from high,
As twinkling stars wink from the sky.

In this art, where every leaf sways,
The breeze carries laughter in playful ways.
Nature's palette, a whimsical spree,
Bringing joy, oh, so effortlessly!

Serenade of the Spruce

In a forest where the squirrels prance,
The spruce trees giggle in a leafy dance.
With branches swaying in playful glee,
They toss acorns down, oh woe is me!

Beneath their shade, the rabbits dart,
Playing tag with a worm—oh, what an art!
They leap and spin, without a care,
Telling tales in the rustling air.

Birds on a branch sing silly tunes,
Challenging the bees to join in swoons.
With a titter and a chirp, they weave,
A symphony of nonsense—who'd believe?

As twilight falls, the stars peek through,
And the spruce keep laughing with their crew.
In nature's throne, the humor's free,
A ballet of quirks beneath the tree.

The Song of the Stray

A scruffy dog with a crooked tail,
Sings off-key in the bright sunlight's veil.
Chasing its shadow down the lane,
It trips on a stick, then starts again.

With a wink and wag, it greets the cats,
Who yawn and stretch on their sunny mats.
They roll their eyes at the foolish pup,
While dreaming of naps and a gentle sup.

The stray struts forth with a joyful bark,
Inviting friends for a stroll in the park.
Through puddles they splash, oh what a sight,
Making mud pies, a pure delight!

At dusk they gather for a round of cheer,
Exchanging stories from the past year.
In laughter and howls, their friendship holds,
A motley crew in the evening gold.

Melodies Among the Moss

In the glen where soft moss grows,
The frogs take turns in melodic shows.
With ribbits high and croaks so deep,
They harmonize, while the fireflies leap.

A snail with dreams of becoming a star,
Slides off on a leaf, oh how bizarre!
It wiggles and jiggles, making a fuss,
But slips and slides into the mossy bus.

The mushrooms nod to the tunes so spry,
While a woodpecker drums, oh my, oh my!
Each note a giggle in the vale,
As nature chuckles, setting the sail.

As dusk turns the world a soft shade,
The woodland joins this grand parade.
With leaves a-clap and a breeze that sings,
They dance through the night on soft, green wings.

Nature's Loyal Lament

The old oak sighs in the gentle breeze,
Its leaves a-whisper with tales like these:
Of acorns dropped and squirrels at play,
Wondering, 'Is it winter or just a grey day?'

A hedgehog rolls with a grunt and a snort,
Lamenting its prickle in a comical sport.
"Why must I cuddle in prickly fright?
I only want warmth, not a poke-attack fight!"

The sunflowers lean, with faces so bright,
As ants march by in a clumsy plight.
They fumble and tumble, a robust parade,
In their tiny world, happy and unafraid.

With evening's glow, the forest chuckles,
As crickets tune up, trading their buckles.
Though nature laments, it's all in good fun,
In this wacky world, we're all on the run!

Reflexions in the Roots

In the garden where dogs dig,
Their noses deep, they dance a jig.
With muddy paws and happy snouts,
They spin around and shake it out.

A squirrel shimmies up the tree,
While barking booms like a symphony.
The roots are tangled, oh what a mess,
Yet laughter blooms, I must confess.

A daffodil bows, so refined,
While canines prance, not far behind.
Their tails like flags in a breezy race,
Nature chuckles at this furry grace.

Calypso of the Canine

A pup in shades, with swagger so bright,
He struts down the block, all day and night.
With every bounce and playful scoff,
He makes the world spin, a doggy boss.

The mailman runs, the kids all giggle,
While the pup does a wiggly wiggle.
A calypso beat as he chases his tail,
Unruly joy never seems to fail.

With twinkling eyes and a woofy grin,
He captures hearts with every spin.
The world a stage, a comedy show,
Where every bark steals a friendly hello.

The Lyrical Leash

With a leash in hand, adventure awaits,
As paws patter along the gates.
A melody of barks fills the air,
With fuzzy companions, no time to spare.

On every corner, a story unfolds,
As mischief and laughter take hold.
The funny noses seek out the smells,
While against the trees, a witty tale swells.

They prance and play, an orchestra's song,
To the rhythm of life where they belong.
Humor in yaps, a symphonic delight,
Dancing through days, both silly and bright.

Tale of the Treetop Whisper

In branches above, a parrot bright,
Chirps down loud to the dogs in delight.
They tilt their heads in a puzzled trance,
Wondering if they should bark or prance.

The tree seems to chuckle, its leaves all sway,
As the dogs below just dream and play.
With a bounce and romp, they all unite,
Creating a ruckus, a funny sight.

As stories flutter from high to low,
The dogs perform in a clever show.
With tail wags and barks, they act like peers,
Filling the woods with laughter and cheers.

Canine Verses Beneath the Stars

Under twinkling skies so wide,
Paws tap dance, tails wag with pride.
Chasing dreams through the grassy lanes,
Whispers of laughter, no room for chains.

Moonlight winks, a playful tease,
Furry dancers sway with ease.
Noses twitch at scents unknown,
Every bark is a joyful tone.

Shooting stars, a chance to leap,
Into the night where secrets creep.
Chasing shadows, they prance and play,
In a world where dogs rule the day.

With each howl, a story spun,
Furry comrades having fun.
Underneath the vast night's dome,
In this magic, they find home.

Symphony of Shadows and Snouts

In the garden, shadows prance,
Snouts investigate, the world's a dance.
Whiskers twitch in the evening air,
Laughter echoes everywhere.

Barking chords of a joyful tune,
Echoes bouncin' beneath the moon.
Paws tap softly on the ground,
Each step plays a happy sound.

Chasing tails, a dizzy whirl,
Four-footed wonders twist and twirl.
Every yip, a note of glee,
In their symphony, pure harmony.

Underneath the stars so bright,
A concert of fur, a playful sight.
With each woof, the night ignites,
In this orchestra of canine flights.

Rhythms of the Rustling Leaves

Through the forest, paws padding light,
Rustling leaves, a curious sight.
Squirrels scamper, a playful tease,
And canine friends bound with ease.

Branches sway with a gentle tune,
While dogs leap beneath the moon.
Every bark, a playful shout,
Nature's hint to join the rout.

Wagging tails in the autumn breeze,
Puppies frolic with such ease.
In the dance of color and sound,
Their joy, a treasure to be found.

With each leap and joyful race,
They craft a rhythm, a lively pace.
In the symphony of leaves and barks,
They chase the magic till it sparks.

The Heartbeat of the Hills

Up in the hills where the green grass sways,
Canine voices play their praise.
A chorus of howls, a playful spree,
Each bark rings home like a melody.

Rolling down in a goofy dash,
Over rocks with a joyful crash.
Paws scatter, laughter fills the air,
Chasing scents without a care.

Sunlight dapples, shadows blend,
Furry pals just around the bend.
With every leap and wagging tail,
Their hearts scream joy; they cannot fail.

In the pulse of hills, they leap so high,
Silly moments like clouds floating by.
With every adventure, their spirits twirl,
Canine dreams in a vibrant whirl.

Harmony of the Hounds

In the park, they race and play,
Chasing tails in a wild ballet.
Paws a-patter, laughter so clear,
Silly snouts full of summer cheer.

A squirrel darts, a leash goes flying,
With one big leap, they're off, undying.
Wagging tails like flags unfurled,
The joy of pups lights up the world.

Tennis balls soar through the breeze,
They leap and tumble, oh what ease!
Furry friends in a rambunctious crew,
Each bark a note in a tune so true.

When the sun sets, their antics fade,
Dreaming of games in the glade.
Harmony lives in each playful bark,
A symphony grown from a little spark.

Echoes of Eternity in the Evergreens

Under the boughs, the dogs convene,
With wagging tails, they're quite the scene.
They snuffle 'neath leaves, find treasures untold,
Chasing shadows as daylight turns gold.

Their howls become whispers, secrets to share,
With a flick of a tail and a jubilant stare.
In this forest, where laughter is keen,
Echoes of joy weave through branches of green.

Rolling in mud, oh what a delight,
Snuggled in pine, they dream of the night.
With each little snort and bouncy retreat,
Every adventure turns into a treat.

As twilight descends, shadows dance high,
They tuck into beds with a soft, sleepy sigh.
Whispers of joy from their dreams take flight,
In the echoes of evening, all feels just right.

The Dogwood's Delight

In the bloom, the pups frolic and dash,
Splashes of petals, a colorful splash.
They leap like dancers in a joyous spree,
Catching the breeze, so wild and free.

With a bark and a nudge, they gather their crew,
Rolling in blossoms, a raucous few.
Each wag of the tail flutters blossoms to ground,
In this fragrant garden, laughter is found.

Chasing butterflies, oh what a sight!
Paws in the air, chasing pure delight.
Every bark a laugh, every pounce a grin,
In the warmth of the sun, their day will begin.

As the day fades and stars peek through,
Dreams of the dogwood dance in blue.
With snuggles and snores, the fun won't depart,
For the joy of their play lives deep in the heart.

Lament of the Lost Trail

Oh where is the path we followed so wide?
The barks and the yips took us for a ride.
Wandering hounds with noses to ground,
Each twist and turn makes laughter abound.

A sniff and a snort lead off the way,
With the scent of adventure, they gambol and sway.
But now they're lost, oh what a plight,
In search of the trail in the fading light.

Frisking through thickets, jumping with glee,
Searching for friends, what happened to we?
With a woof and a wag, they make a new plan,
Chasing each other like only they can.

In the thickets, they find their return,
With barks of joy, for the lesson they learn.
For trails may be lost, but joy will prevail,
In the laughter and love of a wild puppy trail.

Canopy Cantatas

In the leaves, a squirrel sings,
A melody that gently stings.
With nuts in tow, it twirls around,
A furry dancer, quite profound.

Underneath, a rabbit hops,
As clumsy as it surely flops.
With every leap, a twig does snap,
A merry sound, a joyful clap.

Ode to the winds that rustle high,
While birds exchange a cheeky sigh.
Each note a giggle, each breeze a tease,
Nature's jest, the heart's own ease.

So join the fun, sing loud and clear,
In this leafy stage, we hold dear.
Let laughter echo through the air,
A symphony beyond compare.

The Patina of Pine and Poem

In the woods, the pines do grin,
A tree with tales both thick and thin.
With branches swaying, creaky sounds,
Their whispering jokes bounce around.

Underneath, a clever fox,
Juggles acorns in colorful frocks.
With each quick flip, it steals the show,
Nature's clown, oh how they glow!

A chipmunk's quip, a bear's big laugh,
With every joke, they share a gaffe.
And when the sun sets low and red,
The forest teems with humor spread.

Let's raise a cheer to nature's jest,
In every leaf, we find the best.
A patina of laughter shines,
In whispered tales, our joy entwines.